The Beginner's Bible®

★ Animals ★
of the Bible

Sticker & Activity Book

ZONDERkidz

Copyright © 2023 by Zonderkidz

Requests for information should be addressed to:
Zonderkidz, 3900 Sparks Drive SE, Grand Rapids, Michigan 49546

ISBN 978-0-310-14156-3

Design: Diane Mielke

Printed in the United States

23 24 25 26 27 /CWM/ 6 5 4 3 2 1

God Made the Animals

Look at God's creation! Add stickers to finish the picture.

Adam Names the Animals

God made the animals. Adam's job was to name the animals.
Draw a line to match the animal to its name. Then write the animal word yourself.

bee

fish

dog

frog

cat

duck

bird

lion

The Animals Came Two by Two

God's friend Noah built an ark. Animals came two by two and got in the ark.
Add animal stickers to complete the scene.

How many pairs of
animals do you see?

Big or Small

Circle the animal in each box that is BIG. Put an X on the animal that is SMALL.

Animal Patterns

Look at each pattern. Decide which 2 animals come next. Use stickers to complete the pattern.

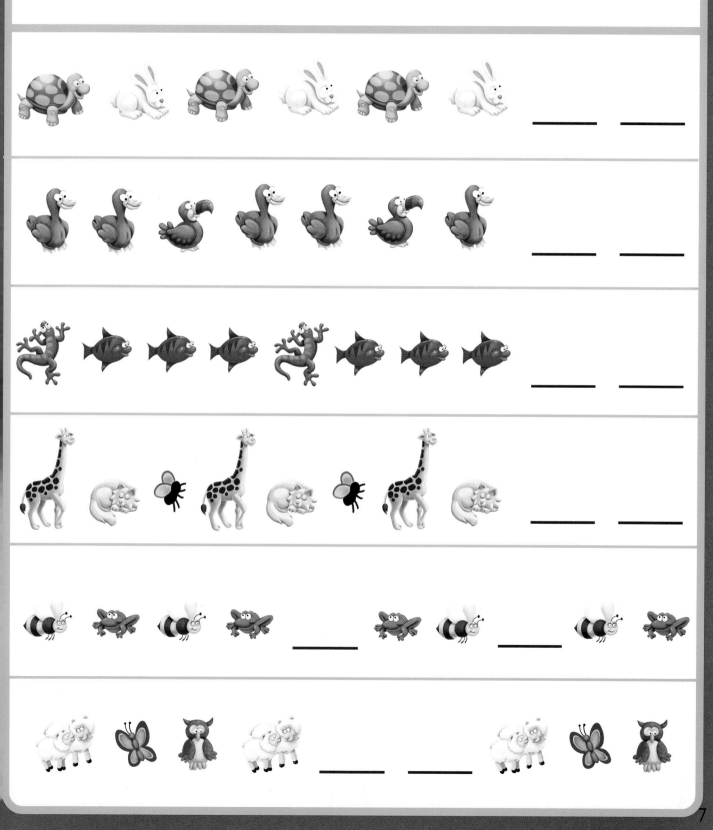

David the Shepherd

When King David was a boy, he was a shepherd. That means he took very good care of sheep. Using stickers, add 7 more sheep to the field David is watching over. He will take good care of them!

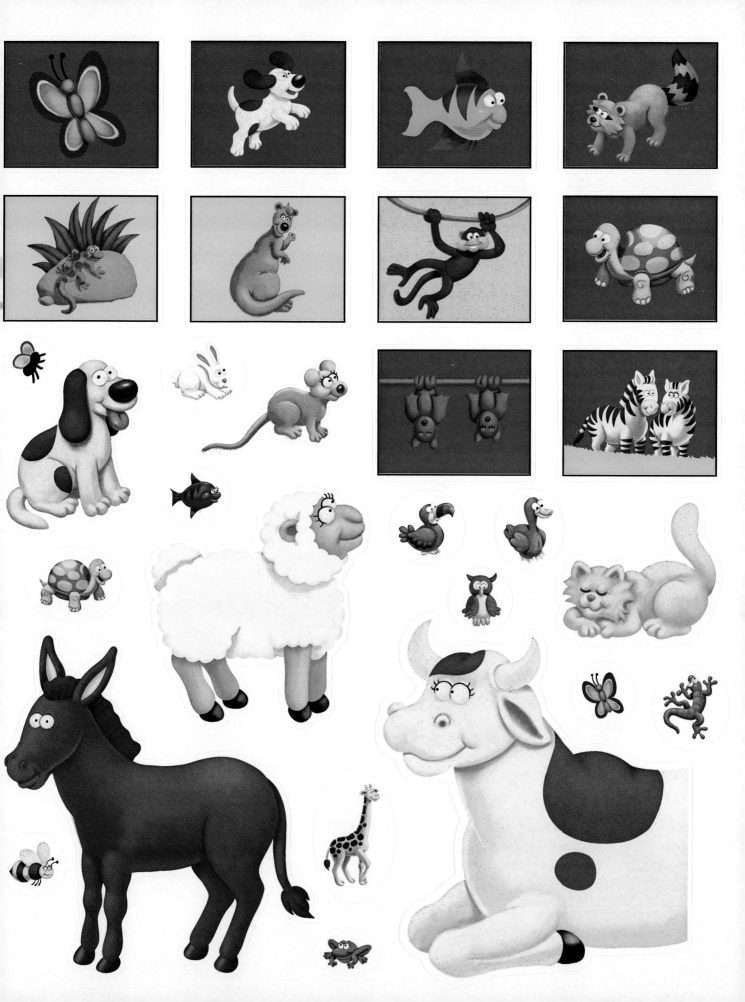

Do You See the Difference?

Daniel was thrown in the lions' den because he prayed to God. He was not afraid of the lions! They did not hurt Daniel. Now look closely. Can you see 8 differences in the pictures below? Circle them.

Bible Animal ABCs

Say the alphabet. Say the animal names too!
Find the animal stickers to help finish the ABCs.

Aa ANT

Bb BUTTERFLY

Cc CAT

Dd DOG

Ee ELEPHANT

Ff FISH

Gg GOAT

Hh HORSE

Ii IGUANA

Jj JELLYFISH

Kk KANGAROO

Ll LION

Mm MONKEY

Nn NIGHT HAWK

Oo OSTRICH

Pp PENGUIN

Qq QUEEN BEE

Rr RACCOON

Ss SPIDER

Tt TURTLE

Uu URCHIN

Vv VAMPIRE BAT

Ww WORM

Xx OX

Yy YELLOW CRAB

Zz ZEBRA

THE END

The Big Fish and Jonah

The big fish spit Jonah out onto the shore near Nineveh.
Now help Jonah go through the maze to the city.

Start

Nineveh

In the Stable

Baby Jesus was born in a stable.

There were animals there to help greet the new baby King.

Add the animal stickers to complete the scene.

Now add a dog, mouse, and donkey sticker wherever you want in the stable.

Donkey Dot-to-Dot

This donkey helped Jesus. He gave him a ride into Jerusalem on Palm Sunday.
Follow the white outline and connect the dots. Color to finish the picture.

14

Bible Animal Crossword

Read the clues about animals in the Bible.
Use the word bank to solve the crossword puzzle.

ACROSS

1. This bird found an olive branch for Noah.

2. Daniel was thrown into a den with this animal when he was caught praying to God.

3. A shepherd takes very good care of these animals.

4. The wise men may have ridden on this animal while looking for baby Jesus.

DOWN

1. Jesus rode this animal into Jerusalem on Palm Sunday.

3. The devil looked like this animal when he tempted Adam and Eve in the garden.

WORD BANK

Snake

Lion

Camel

Dove

Donkey

Sheep

Animal Word Search

There are lots of animals in the Bible!
Use the word bank below. Find and circle the animal names in the word search.
Words can go in any direction!

LION

FISH

SNAKE

HORSE

DONKEY

SHEEP

LAMB

DOVE

QUAIL

FROG

OXEN

CAMEL

BEE

LOCUST

H	S	I	F	K	Y	R	T	E	L	U	V	Q	L	B
Y	V	G	G	E	K	O	B	H	K	H	Y	I	Y	Y
P	A	O	K	C	H	A	N	L	I	A	O	F	P	R
X	Z	N	U	W	O	F	X	E	V	N	N	D	H	L
L	O	C	U	S	T	E	Z	H	A	S	R	S	V	U
D	L	Q	J	V	E	L	D	T	P	M	Y	A	Y	J
U	E	F	E	B	J	G	O	R	F	S	H	E	E	P
P	M	G	S	N	G	V	V	W	Q	F	F	Y	Y	M
V	A	G	R	G	E	F	E	A	Q	X	X	O	U	M
S	C	F	O	A	L	X	A	I	R	M	F	S	R	W
B	E	O	H	L	F	F	O	E	O	J	S	S	Q	D
L	E	P	H	W	L	J	N	V	F	Y	V	U	C	Q
M	A	H	Y	X	R	O	E	G	H	J	A	S	B	N
Z	K	M	T	Y	S	C	J	B	B	I	F	W	F	I
T	V	F	B	T	I	G	J	B	L	C	R	G	Z	E